AIR STRUCTURES

Published in 2015 by
Laurence King Publishing Ltd
361–373 City Road
London EC1V 1LR
United Kingdom
email: enquiries@laurenceking.com
www.laurenceking.com

A catalogue record for this book
is available from the British Library

ISBN: 978 1 78067 482 7

Design by & SMITH
Cover designed by Pentagram

Printed in China

Will McLean and Pete Silver teach at the Faculty of
Architecture and the Built Environment at the University
of Westminster and are the co-authors of *Fabrication:
The Designers Guide* (2006), *Introduction to Architectural
Technology* (2013), and *Structural Engineering for
Architects* (2014).

Air
Structures

WILL MCLEAN & PETE SILVER

LAURENCE KING PUBLISHING

I LIKE AIR STRUCTURES BECAUSE THE MAJOR STRUCTURAL ELEMENT YOU CAN BREATHE AND IT SMELLS OF VIOLETS AND YOU CAN'T DRAW IT.

Cedric Price, 1984

CONTENTS

3.0

AIR: DESIGNING AND FABRICATING

4.0

THE TECHNOLOGY OF AIR

AIR STRUCTURES: A HISTORY

'Pneumatics is the forming process of all living things'

GRAHAM STEVENS
Desert Cloud, 1974

Air Structures presents an eclectic survey of buildings, engineering structures, sculpture, furniture and other utilities, where the use of air is the key structural, motive or generative element. Air structures are often viewed as a niche area of the building arts, this sourcebook encourages the reader to explore their potential and the inexpensive and plentiful 'material' of pressurized air. Against a backdrop of environmental imperatives which, as Richard Buckminster Fuller usefully reminds us, suggest we 'do more with less', the examples in this book hopefully illustrate the immense structural and environmental properties of differential air pressure and the myriad artefactual possibilities.

The book is divided into three main sections. The first, 'Air: Structures', illustrates the primary types of inflatable structures and includes large-span (air supported) exhibition spaces, smaller (air cell and air beam) buildings and other pneumatic products, including environmental sculpture and bridges. The following section entitled 'Air: Movement' illustrates how air can be used to create movement and replace the heavier engineering of a piston actuator with the softer – but no less powerful – air muscle; or the air cushion technology of the Air Caster, for heavy lifting and transportation.

'The air structure is the most efficient structural form available to date ... no other type of structure has the potential of providing free-span coverage for so large an area ... as the air structure is constructed of light-weight, flexible materials, it can be made easily portable and lends itself readily to the design of demountable or removable structures.'

WALTER BIRD, 1967

Walter Bird stands atop his inflatable 'radome' on the Cornell Aeronautical Laboratory grounds, Buffalo, New York, 1948.

The third section, 'Air: Designing and Fabricating',
investigates how we might use air as a design tool
through the study of soap-film models pioneered
by Frei Otto, or use air as the forming medium in the
development of products and materials such as Oskar
Zieta's Plopp stool or Dante Bini's inflated concrete
shell structures. These three sections are followed by
a brief note on the basic principle and measurement
of air pressure, and some biographies of key academics,
engineers and architects who have contributed to the
development of air structures.

Almost 50 years ago Dante Bini participated in a
remarkable event held at the University of Stuttgart
that was hosted by Frei Otto; the *1st International
Colloquium on Pneumatic Structures* (1967). The
colloquium welcomed the leaders of this rapidly evolving
technological art, which included Walter Bird, Victor
Lundy, Heinz Isler, Dante Bini, Nikolaus Laing and Cedric
Price. Walter Bird presented an overview of the field,
entitled *The Development of Pneumatic Structures, Past
Present and Future*. Bird had constructed the world's first

*Standard Pneumatic
Environment,*
Graham Stevens, 1968.

air-supported radar cover (or radome) in 1946 and in 1955 he established Birdair Structures to commercialize his inventions, which included pneumatic 'bubble' enclosures for tennis courts and swimming pools. He attracted much media attention. Birdair subsequently produced large-scale pneumatic structures (notably with architect Victor Lundy) and led this field through developments of materials and fabrication techniques.

Visual artist Graham Stevens had attended the Stuttgart event and was particularly interested in the structure and science of these new forms. Stevens began to create his own pneumatic artworks, exploring how new kinds of environmental art and enclosure could be made against the backdrop of heightened political, social and environmental awareness at the end of the 1960s. The inexpensive power and potential of air to create structure and to moderate environments suggested new modes of climatic envelopes and a redefinition of the physical interaction between architecture, occupant and environment.

Atmosfield,
St. Katharine Docks,
Graham Stevens, 1970.

A more recent development of the pneumatic membrane as a building skin is the ETFE cushion. The air-filled pillows of Vector Foiltec's Ethylene Tetrafluoroethylene (ETFE) constitute a disruptive technology that has been introduced to the construction industry by architect Ben Morris. In large-scale roof and cladding projects, glazed elements can be replaced with large ETFE cushions at a fraction of the weight and with attendant structural economies. If you extend this thinking across a large-scale housing development, then priorities for thermal insulation and heating systems can be re-ordered and you return to Buckminster Fuller's pioneering idea of domed-over cities. (In 1950, Fuller proposed a 2-mile (3.2-km) diameter dome or 'bubble' over mid-Manhattan to obviate expensive heating and cooling across the city and that, he claimed, would have paid for itself in ten years.) ETFE is typically used as multi-layered inflated cushions with low air pressure. This resists the natural creep of the material and structurally stiffens the panels. The layering of the cushions can also be used to create active (deployable) internal surfaces that can control opacity or allow responsive thermal performance.

A recent development in structural pneumatics is Rolf Luchsinger and Mauro Pedretti's Tensairity® structures (see p.74). Tensairity uses the structural efficiency of Buckminster Fuller's tensegrity principle (separating the compressive and tensile elements) and creates a compressive component from an air beam, which is in turn resisted and reinforced by a coaxial winding of steel (tensile) cable. These new lightweight composite beams have been used as bridge structures, temporary enclosures and wide-span roofs. In Luchsinger and Pedretti's paper outlining Tensairity's structural principles and the field of pressure-induced stability, the technology is said to be capable of the load-bearing of a steel beam, with substantial weight reduction.

Atmosfield,
St. Katharine Docks,
Graham Stevens, 1970.

Transmobile, colour experiment,
Graham Stevens, 1968.

The designer Nick Crosbie (co-founder of the design
company Inflate, see p.57) has been working with
inflatable products and structures for over 20 years.
At a recent lecture at the University of Westminster,
London, Crosbie demonstrated the utility and portable
qualities of the genre by inflating an entire changing
room from a backpack in less than a minute. Inflate and
sister company AirClad work at a range of scales, from
their iconic inflatable eggcup to large-scale temporary
'event' buildings that can be very quickly inflated and
deflated. These structures utilize a medium that provides
continuous structural support across a surface (even at
low pressure) as opposed to the more roughly calibrated,
but ubiquitous support of beams and columns.

Pneumatic Environment, Paris Biennale,
Graham Stevens, 1971.

The UK government report *Air Structures: A Survey*,
co-authored by architect Cedric Price and structural
engineers Frank Newby and Robert Suan, was published
in 1971 and still represents the most comprehensive
survey of pneumatic structures and their technology.
Inspired by this report, this book re-visits the world
of air structures and looks at current developments,
as well as some spectacular historical projects.
The whiff of novelty seems to hamper, or at least limit the
extent of air structures in architecture. Designers should
take inspiration from the high-tech industries of the
nautical and aeronautical, where constantly improved
performance requirements demands new design
approaches and materials technologies. Architecture
and the building-enclosure businesses should be no
different and – as the success of ETFE cushions has
proved – innovation in the construction industry with
the use of air structures is demonstrably achievable.

AIR: STRUCTURES

1.1 / AIR-SUPPORTED STRUCTURES

Air-supported structures are typically fabric membrane enclosures anchored to the ground around the perimeter, and held aloft by low pressure pumped into the structure via air blowers or fan units. While this type of structure uses airlocks (often with two sets of doors) to prevent a sudden drop in pressure, they are 'leaky' and so require constant or intermittent air to top-up the relative internal pressure. The internal pressure can be increased to resist strong winds or snow loads.

Pavilions for the 12th World Orchid Conference
Yutaka Murata and Mamoru Kawaguchi
Kanagawa, Japan. 1987

Both pavilions are single-skinned, cable restrained, air-supported structures. The circular pavilion has a diameter of 75 m (246 ft) and rises to a height at the apex of 19.5 m (64 ft). The pavilion is reinforced by a two-way wire rope 'cable net' on a 5 m (16 ft) grid. Kawaguchi's great innovation was to introduce a secondary reinforcing mesh of fishing net. This net, on a 100 mm (3.87 in.) grid allows the airtight skin to be formed with a very thin and inexpensive layer of transparent PVC film, only 0.1 mm (0.003 in.) thick.

The tight grid of the fishing net avoids any significant stresses on the PVC film and obviates the need for expensive pattern-cut and tailored fabric. The second pavilion is shaped like a caterpillar and is 40-m (131-ft) wide and 100-m (328-ft) long. This structure is also reinforced with wire ropes (in transverse and radial directions), with longitudinal reinforcement along the ridge. Both pavilions use double-door airlocks to maintain the internal pressure that supports these enormous structures.

Above: Aerial view of the pavilions.

Left: Pavilion 1 is prepared for inflation. Both the fishing-net mesh and the cable net (in black) are visible. In the background of the image the prefabricated double-door airlock can be seen.

Inflation begins.
Airlock tube entrances
are visible to the left
of the image. Next,
the large dome is lifted
off the ground with
low-pressure air.
The cable net is now
clearly visible.

Interior of an agricultural air dome,
also by Murata and Kawaguchi.
The image clearly illustrates the
hierarchy of structure with a grid of
cables (clamped at their intersection)
defining the key geometries, while
the 100 mm (3.87 in.) fishing-net grid
holds the (almost invisible) plastic film.

Oase No. 7
Haus-Rucker-Co
Kassel, Germany. 1972

Documenta is an exhibition of contemporary art held every
five years in Kassel, Germany. As part of documenta 5, the
avant-garde Viennese architecture collective of Haus-Rucker-Co
created an 8-m (26-ft) diameter transparent protuberance
inflated out of the facade of the Fridericianum museum. A tubular
steel space-frame deck connects through the window opening
and acts as a cantilevered deck on which a circular steel frame
supports the clear PVC sphere. A small air blower pressurizes the
bubble and air pressure is maintained by using zips on the inside
edge that form an airlock. The 'oasis' featured a pair of fake palm
trees with plastic leaves, with a hammock strung between them
for the single-occupant castaway.

Lange House Cover
Haus-Rucker-Co
Krefeld, Germany. 1971

As part of a site-specific artwork entitled *Cover*, the architects
Haus-Rucker-Co created an inflated translucent membrane
that entirely covered Mies van der Rohe's 1921 Lange House
in Krefeld. The architects, speculating on future environmental
pollution, described the resulting, temporary structure: 'In
the interior, the light, evenly filtered through the shell from all
sides, created a pallid hothouse atmosphere in which not only
the garden plants started to change but also the proportions of
the house itself.' Fabricated from translucent, reinforced PVC,
a hemispherical cross-section follows the footprint of the building.
With the rounded corners of an inflatable structure, the project
forms a heart shape in plan.

Spacebuster
Raumlaborberlin
New York City. 2009

'Spacebuster was developed and designed to explore the public space in New York City. As a research tool it acts as a transformer of the architectural and the social space, i.e. the urban space.'

RAUMLABORBERLIN

Commissioned by New York's Storefront Gallery, Spacebuster was a travelling conversation and learning space that literally operated out the back of a van or, in this case, a US utility truck. A single-skin polythene bubble was inflated out of the back of a truck at a series of event locations across Manhattan and Brooklyn. The inflated space created could house up to 80 people and the translucent skin offered its visitors an enclosure while maintaining a view of their surroundings – and some incidental theatre for onlookers and passers-by.

Spacebuster at an event in New York City.

Sketch of the Spacebuster concept.

Interior photograph of the Airhall
showing its 'net' of cables.

Coolhurst Tennis Airhall
Birds Portchmouth Russum
London, UK. 2006

This single-skin, air-supported dome uses low, fan-assisted air pressure, maintained by a double set of doors that form an airlock. The Airhall is a demountable structure covering two tennis courts. It is inflated during the winter to protect the courts against the weather. The Airhall has a robust, reinforced white PVC perimeter skirt with a translucent PVC crown that allows natural light to enter during the day and the existing tennis floodlighting to illuminate the hall at night. The structure can be assembled and demounted over two days. The PVC skin is restrained using a network of exterior cables, which are fixed at regular intervals to pre-installed ground anchors sited around the perimeter of the structure.

Musée Mobile (MuMo)
Adam Kalkin
Europe and Africa. 2010–

This project for a travelling children's museum of contemporary art was designed by American architect Adam Kalkin. It features the art of Daniel Buren, James Turrell, Laurence Weiner and the icon-indicator of Paul McCarthy's giant red inflatable rabbit to let everyone know that this particular art circus has rolled into your town or village. Employing his trademark module of the shipping container, Kalkin uses hydraulic rams to open up the structure and transform it from truck to museum. The Musée Mobile has so far travelled 38,000 km (23,600 miles) from France to Belgium, Switzerland, the Ivory Coast and Cameroon. The Musée is currently travelling across Spain, where it will visit 40 locations and 7,500 schoolchildren. Kalkin has recently launched a subsidiary project called Industrial Zombie, specializing in transforming shipping containers so that they can be used for temporary events, by utilizing hydraulics and giant inflatable airbags.

The Musée Mobile making a visit to Paris.

Ghost Army Decoy Tank
US Army
Various. 1944–1945

During the apogee of World War II, with finances stretched and military hardware scarce, several operations by the Allied armies involved the deployment of inflatable decoys that included tanks and planes. The Ghost Army is a name that was given to a special unit within the US Army whose job was to deceive the German army about relative locations and deployment numbers of troops and munitions. Interestingly, the army unit included visual artists, photographers and designers, notably Ellsworth Kelly, Bill Blass and Art Kane. Using inflatable 'decoy' munitions alongside the simulated sounds of troop movements and other such theatrical fakery, they gained much-needed advantage for the Allied forces. Rick Beyer's excellent documentary film *The Ghost Army* features original colour footage and interviews with veterans of the project.

Atmosfield
Graham Stevens
London, UK. 1970

'The Atmosfield demonstrates a controlled use of natural forces with direct implication for living environments. The Atmosfield was extended across the water by "walking on water" tubes and into the air by an early version of the Atmospheric Raft, which contained helium.'

GRAHAM STEVENS

Stevens is a fine artist, however, he works across the domain of architecture and the acquisition of his early drawings by the Centre Pompidou is under the auspices of 'experimental architecture'. Stevens began working with air structures and plastic membranes to explore the idea of a colour-saturated environment as an inhabitable artwork: the structure formed by the air, the colour by the fabric. Stevens swiftly realized that air and fabric were a very quick, lightweight and inexpensive means to create structures and environments, and the success of his early prototypes encouraged him to purchase his own high-frequency welding machine to connect the plastic membranes. His studio in London's then semi-derelict St. Katharine Docks became the site for a series of extraordinary large-scale air sculptures, brilliantly captured on film by photographer Andrew Tweedie.

1.2 / AIR-BEAM STRUCTURES

An air beam is an air-inflated tube that acts as a beam or arch to give support in a fabric structure. Using a series of parallel, conjoined air beams, large-spanning enclosures can be created. Air beams can be either high- or low-pressure components. Low-pressure air beams – such as the beams used to support AZC's Peace Pavilion (see p.36) – operate at pressures as low as 16 kPa (2.320 psi) and often require a constant or intermittent air source to top up the pressure. High-pressure air beams are more akin to a pneumatic tyre, where the beam is pressurized and has a valve for occasional maintenance.

The fabrication process of an air beam – the PVC-coated woven fabric is stitched and bonded with adhesives. The fabric is doubled up to strengthen areas around air-inlet valves and edges.

Fuji Pavilion
Yutaka Murata and Mamoru Kawaguchi
Osaka, Japan. 1970

The Fuji Group Pavilion for Expo '70 was the largest air-inflated structure in the world when it was built. Circular in plan and 50 m (164 ft) in diameter, the structure was formed of 16 tubular arches, each with a cross-sectional diameter of 4 m (13 ft). The two central arches have a semi-circular profile, but – as the distance between the two footings of each arch becomes closer in plan – the arches become higher toward the ends of the pavilion. As Kawaguchi explains, 'This principle affords a shape to the building that is unique and perfectly defined by geometry.' The air pressure inside the tubes was kept at about 7.8 kPa (1.131 psi) which could be increased to 24.5 kPa (3.5 psi) to resist storm conditions. The structure was surrounded by multi-coloured Binishell domes (see p.115) that were decorated by dropping paint from a helicopter.

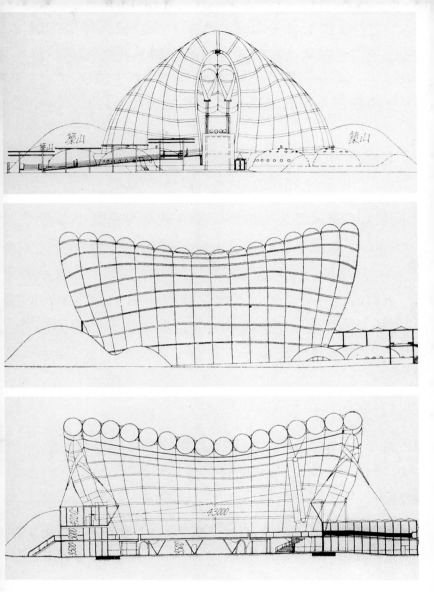

Peace Pavilion
Atelier Zündel Cristea (AZC)
London, UK. 2013

The Peace Pavilion was exhibited in
Museum Gardens in East London's
Bethnal Green during the summer of 2013.
The pavilion represents 'peace ... as one
of the highest human ideals', and the
designers used a single symmetrical line
of tailored inflated tube; lifted up and held
down to ground, to explore the blurring
of 'our notions of the inside and outside'.
4-m (13-ft) high and designed only with
PVC membrane and air, it is a self-
supporting structure made of inflated
air beams. Its rain cover of clear PVC is
zipped into place. To achieve such an
apparently complex shape, the designers
used parametric design tools and the
study of tensile membranes to create
doubly curved surfaces. The pressure
needed to maintain the inflated tubular
structure is just 18 – 16 kPa (2.6 – 2.3 psi)
and its energy consumption is equivalent
to that of a sandwich toaster.

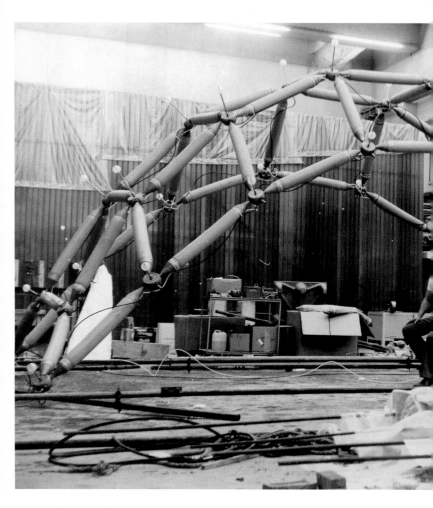

Angus Brown's Loose Geometry
and Memory Joint project.

Loose Geometry:
Memory Joints
Angus Brown
University of Westminster, London.
1975

A geodesic structure is created with a series of inflated members forming the struts. Angus Brown's Loose Geometry project explored how the effectiveness of geodesic frame structures for temporary events and shelters could be improved with the use of a universal 'Memory Joint'. A 12-node ball-and-socket connector was designed to accept structural members from all directions and be mechanically set to 'memorize' their positions. The inflatable struts were developed to significantly lighten the overall frame and their development was sponsored by the chemical company and composites specialists Scott Bader.

Canopy Raft

Dany Cleyet-Marrel, Gilles Ebersolt
Guyana, Cameroon, Madagascar and Gabon. 1989 –

An initiative of Francis Hallé, Dany Cleyet-Marrel and Gilles Ebersolt, this structure forms a mobile scientific laboratory that includes an overnight shelter and storage facilities. The entire structure is designed to be lifted by hot-air balloon and deposited on water or, most notably, the canopy of a rainforest. The rainforest canopy, which is almost impossible to access from ground level, can then be fully explored by scientists operating from this flexible working platform of pneumatically inflated air beams and nylon mesh. The canopies are gently lowered into place and left (with scientists) to be collected the following day.

1.3 / AIR-CELL STRUCTURES

An air-cell structure is an air-inflated, double-skin, low-pressure inflatable where two membranes are connected with ties or diaphragm webs to form double-surface quilts rigidized with air. The fabric is held in place under tension from the internal, compressive force of air under pressure, while the cellular nature of the structure offers an enormous range of geometric variations, including the capacity to be self-supporting and to resist wind load. Air-cell structures require points of stiffening and reinforcing, either for intrinsic structural reasons or for connections, e.g. tethering and anchorage. They also require connections for air intake and extraction. The fans used in air cell-structures normally operate on full power during inflation, but will then switch to intermittent mode and react only in response to a drop in pressure. While some of these structures look similar to air-beam structures, the air cells are cross-connected and are not separately pressurized.

Bubble Wrap® was invented by the Sealed Air Corporation in 1960. It was originally intended to be used as a type of textured wallpaper, but the inventors quickly realized it was an excellent cushioning material, and Sealed Air is now a global company.

METHOD FOR MAKING LAMINATED CUSHIONING MATERIAL

Filed Nov. 27, 1959　　　　　　　　　　　　3 Sheets—Sheet 2

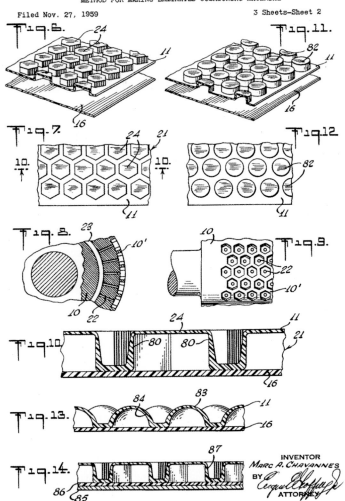

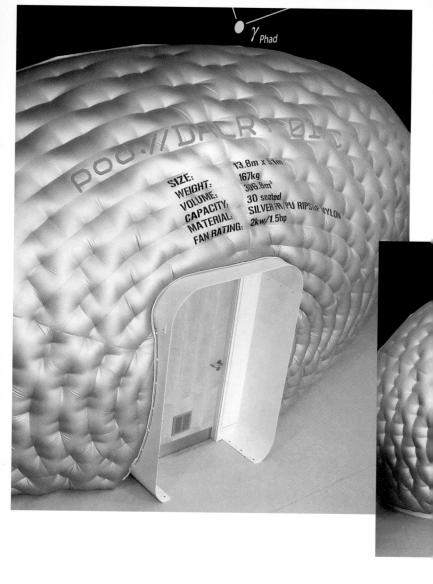

γ Phad

pod.//DAERY01C

SIZE: 13.8m x 5.1m
WEIGHT: 167kg
VOLUME: 306.3m³
CAPACITY: 30 seated
MATERIAL: SILVER FR/PU RIPSTOP NYLON
FAN RATING: 2kw/1.5hp

Dalry Primary School Pod
Bruce McLean, Will McLean and Inflate
Dalry, Scotland. 2007

One of seven specially designed classrooms for the new Dalry
Primary School, the school's computing facility is housed within
an inflatable pod. The school wanted to provide a dedicated
space for students to learn about computing that was something
more innovative than a rigid classroom. This soft, cocoon-like
inflatable structure provides an area of both visual and acoustic
separation. It is nicknamed 'the brain' by pupils. The low pressure
within the double-skinned inflatable quilt is kept topped-up
by a low-powered fan unit. The markings on the outside of the
structure describe its technical specifications, including its weight,
dimensions and relative air pressure.

Inflatable Exhibition Wall
Will McLean and Inflate
Venice, Italy. 2014

This 6-m (19-ft 8-in.) long and 2.4-m
(7-ft 10-in.) high exhibition wall uses
a structural system developed by
Nick Crosbie at Inflate. Crosbie's
'Bonewall' system is designed to be
self-supporting with 'flared' ends,
forming a 'bone' shape in plan. The wall
is made from rip-stop nylon, sections
of which are stitched together, and
includes a small 100-watt fan unit that is
attached by Velcro to the main structure.
The project was commissioned to
celebrate the Sardinian villa built by
Dante Bini for film director Michelangelo
Antonioni and displays photographs of
the building, as well as reproductions
of the original drawings of a house
'built with air' (see p.118). The fabric
is digitally printed before assembly
and is incredibly lightweight; the
whole structure (with fan) weighs in at
an insubstantial 15 kg (33 lb) and was
transported to the Biennale in a small
suitcase. The structure takes just three
minutes to inflate.

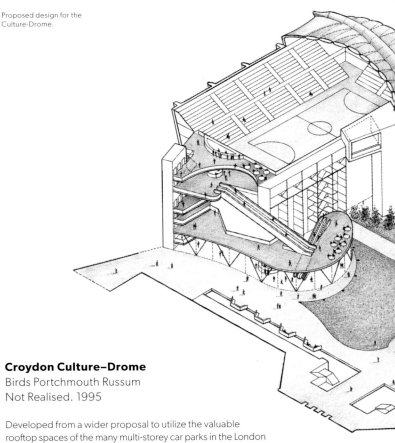

Croydon Culture–Drome
Birds Portchmouth Russum
Not Realised. 1995

Developed from a wider proposal to utilize the valuable
rooftop spaces of the many multi-storey car parks in the London
suburb of Croydon, Culture-Drome was a detailed design for a
pneumatic envelope to create a new arts and sports venue. Using
a mixture of fabrics with varying levels of opacity and colour, the
pneumatic structure was to be composed of interconnected
high-pressure air beams. The architects described some of the
project's advantages thus: '…waterproof, provides external and
internal finishes, allows for light penetration (reducing artificial
lighting costs) and would require little maintenance.'

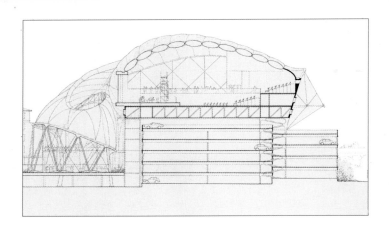

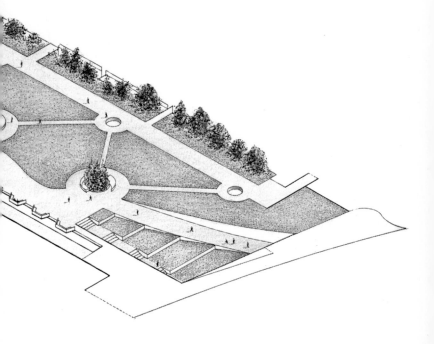

Croydon, The Future. Proposal for a
series of inflatable rooftop structures,
including a 'buoyant' structure.

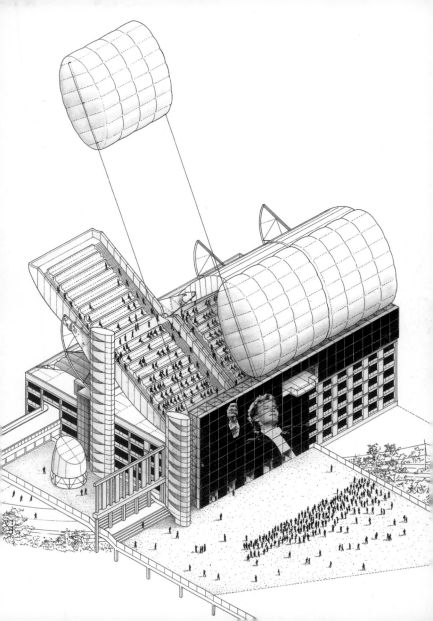

1.4 / AIR CUSHION BUILDING ENVELOPES

In architecture, new lightweight materials technology has enabled the construction of previously utopian visions. For example, Frei Otto and Buckminster Fuller's large city-scale enclosures would now be possible through the use of the Ethylene Tetrafluoroethylene (ETFE) cushions technology pioneered by Vector Foiltec.

ETFE is a man-made fluoropolymer whose principle ingredient is fluorite. ETFE cushion structures use two or more ETFE films – inflated by air – to create a building skin that is waterproof, UV transparent and a lightweight alternative to glass. The cushions use a very low-pressure inflation and top-up system, and by using multiple ETFE layered and printed cushions, and variable air pressure across these layers, a thermally dynamic and responsive building skin can be created. The properties of ETFE compared to glass are impressive: ETFE is 1% of the weight of glass, transmits more light and costs 24–70% less to install. A variety of aluminium sections have been designed to grip the multilayered films and create a framing system for connection to a superstructure.

Media-ICT
Enric Ruiz-Geli, Cloud 9
Barcelona, Spain. 2011

One of the ambitions of this project was to create an environmentally responsible and responsive building. This is illustrated in the two ETFE facades. The southeast facade has an external skin of inflatable ETFE cushions that act as a variable sunscreen, letting in more daylight and sunlight in the winter for solar heat gain, and becoming more opaque in the summer months to protect and shade the building's inhabitants. The opacity of the ETFE skin of the southeast facade is controlled through the differential movement of offset printed films, which, by varying relative internal air pressure, can be moved further together or apart to create solar shade. The southwest facade uses a nitrogen and oil-based fog machine to pump fog into the top of the huge vertical cushions and so control their opacity, creating a translucent facade. This is the first time such a fogging system has been successfully installed as a part of a building skin.

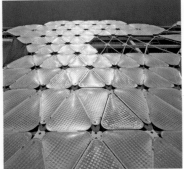

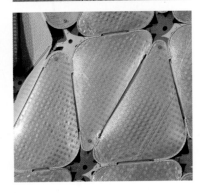

The southeast facade has a responsive external skin of inflatable ETFE cushions.

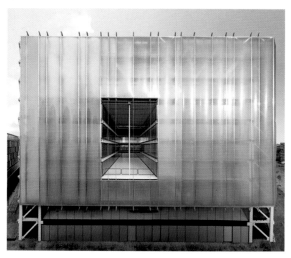

The southwest facade uses a nitrogen and oil-based fog machine to control internal light levels.

An ETFE skin has also been used in the stadium for Basel football club in Switzerland, designed by Herzog & de Meuron.

AirClad Facade System
Nick Crosbie, Inflate
Various. 2009 –

Experimenting with semi-permanent and permanent facade
systems using air, designer Nick Crosbie has developed AirClad.
The system uses low-pressure inflated air cells connected to a
series of structural ribs to create an effect a little like the bellows
of an old camera. The ribs provide an armature for the inflated
membrane windows and roofing of the wraparound skin, while
also providing structural connections for the floor and roof. The
AirClad system has been used to create a variety of structures,
including garden offices, house extensions and demountable
pavilions for education and corporate clients.

AirClad rooftop pavilion.

AirClad lightweight garden building.

AirClad house extension structure
with opaque PVC inflatable skin.

1.5 / BUOYANT AND LIGHTER-THAN-AIR STRUCTURES

Air buoyancy can be achieved by reducing the density of air within a structure. This is the principle by which a hot-air balloon stays airborne, as the heating of air reduces its density and creates lift. Lighter-than-air gases, such as hydrogen or helium, can also be used to create buoyant structures, although the big disadvantage of hydrogen is that it is highly flammable—as witnessed by the *Hindenburg* disaster of 1937. Helium is non-combustible and has provided the buoyant medium for airships for almost 100 years. However, helium is a finite resource and projects like Graham Stevens' Desert Cloud (see p.68), Anam Hasan's tetroon experiments (see p.64) and Buckminster Fuller's Cloud Nine proposal (see p.62) instead use air density differentials—utilizing the heat of the sun—to counteract gravity and literally 'float' structures.

The Roof That Goes Up In Smoke
Overtreders W
Holland. 2010

This buoyant pavilion by Dutch design studio Overtreders W uses a canopy inflated with the hot air produced by a wood-burning stove, which itself forms a focal point and is used to cook chestnuts, soup and hot chocolate for the events that take place there. The project uses the increased buoyancy of hot air to form a canopy that, despite appearances, has to be anchored to the ground, rather than held up from the ground. The design cleverly takes social activities happening within the pavilion (sitting with friends, eating, drinking, keeping warm) and uses the heat generated to create a canopy structure.

Cloud Nine Floating Tensegrity Spheres
Buckminster Fuller with Shoji Sadao
Not Realised. 1958

One of Buckminster Fuller's most ambitious and poetic
proposals was for a series of spherical floating communities
of 1000 people. These large spheres, half a mile (0.8 km) in
diameter are made buoyant by the sun's natural heating of
the air inside these floating 'cloud' communities.

'… a 100-ft-diameter, tensegrity-trussed, geodesic sphere weighing
three tons encloses seven tons of air. The air-to-structural-weight
ratio is two to one. When we double the size so that the geodesic
sphere is 200 ft in diameter, the weight of the structure increases
to seven tons while the weight of the air increases to fifty-six tons
– the air-to-structure ratio changes as eight to one…When we
get to a geodesic sphere one-half mile in diameter, the weight
of the structure itself becomes of relatively negligible magnitude,
for the [air-to-structure] ratio is approximately a thousand to one
… When the interior temperature of the sphere rises only one degree
Fahrenheit, the weight of the air pushed out of the sphere is greater
than the weight of the spherical-frame geodesic structure … the
geodesic sphere and its contained air will have to float outwardly,
into the sky, being displaced by the heavy atmosphere around it.'

RICHARD BUCKMINSTER FULLER,
Critical Path, St. Martin's Press, New York, 1981.

Project Echo
NASA
Various. 1960

The Echo 1 communications balloon was launched in Weeksville, North Carolina, USA, by NASA in 1960 as the world's first communication satellite. A 'passive' satellite, it reflected radio and radar signals from a low earth orbit. Also known as a 'satelloon', a composite of satellite and balloon, Echo 1 was 30.5 m (100 ft) in diameter and weighed only 68 kg (150 lb) with a metalized mylar skin of only 0.5 mm thickness. As a non-rigid, the satellite could only be used at high altitudes, where there is minimal aerodynamic drag.

Tetroons
Anam Hasan
Prototyped in London. 2012

Exploring ideas for temporary festival structures, Hasan has
created large tetrahedral balloons made of black polythene
rubbish bags, all taped together. After wind inflation using the
prevailing breeze, the black surface of the tetrahedron balloon
absorbs the sun's energy and heats the air inside, creating
buoyancy and thus lift.

Inside the black polythene tetroon.

The inflation of the buoyant tetroon.

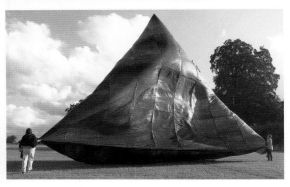

Proposal for a field of buoyant tetroons
for a desert festival.

Desert Cloud
Graham Stevens
Arabian Desert near Kuwait. 1974

Graham Stevens's Desert Cloud is an environmental sculpture
that explores energy transformation and the principle of
buoyancy. A transparent PVC cellular mattress, it is sub-divided
by black membrane webs and lined on the underside with a silver
reflective fabric. This specific arrangement captures the radiation
of the sun through the transparent layer, while the black internal
panels shorten the sun's wavelength, so heating the air inside to
create a buoyant structure or 'cloud'. The reflective underside
provides much-needed shade from the desert sun. Stevens also
demonstrated how the structure could condense (or capture)
water on its surface, even managing to create ice from a clear
desert night sky.

Helium Brick Lifter

Edward Mascarenas and Alastair Ferguson
University of Westminster, London. 2009

Students investigating structural support systems at the University of Westminster devised a novel means of holding a single brick aloft, which employed 200 balloons filled with the inert gas helium. Helium is four times lighter than air and 1000 litres (35.3 cubic feet) of helium can lift approximately a 1 kg (2.2 lbs) weight. Although helium is the second most abundant element in the universe there are worries about an imminent shortage. Helium is a by-product of natural gas production of which worldwide stores have been steadily declining. It is also in demand for use (in liquid form) as the coolant for the superconducting magnets employed in MRI scanners.

1.6 / INFLATABLE BRIDGES, BOOMS AND BUOYS

Lightness, ease of deployment and relatively low cost are three good reasons why air structures are increasingly used as bridging systems, floating booms and buoys. A trapped body of air within a fabric-skinned form creates an excellent lightweight float. Temporary bridging solutions such as the LMCS system developed by the US military (see p.76) marry conventionally engineered aluminium decking sections with inflatable (and thus collapsible) floats, whereas in the case of Atelier Zündel Cristea's (AZC) Paris bridge (opposite), a new kind of soft utility is created where pedestrians can bounce, rather than walk, across the River Seine. The MEXE project (see p.75) from the 1960s shows that the notion of an inflated 'spanning' structure is not new. Rolf Luchsinger's Tensairity Bridge (see p.74) offers an innovative union of structural systems by employing Buckminster Fuller's tensegrity principle of separating compressive and tensile forces. In doing so, Luchsinger has invented a new structural type, the chief component of which is air.

Bouncing Bridge
Atelier Zündel Cristea (AZC)
Paris, France. 2012

Bouncing Bridge is a proposal for an inflatable bridge with giant trampolines that the architects describe as being '...dedicated to the joyful release from gravity as one bounces above the river... The Bouncing Bridge allows every visitor a novel view of Paris from his or her own unique spatial position: upright and leaping, upside down and tumbling, gliding above like a circus performer...'

Sited near the Bir-Hakeim bridge, the Bouncing Bridge concept was to be

formed of three inflatable modules, like giant lifebelts, each 30 m (98 ft) in diameter and held together with cables to form a stable structure. The central section of each ring is a trampoline. Each arch-like module is held in tension with 3700 cubic metres (130,664 cubic feet) of air. Designed specifically of lightweight materials – PVC membrane, trampoline mesh and air – this proposal was designed to cross the Seine at a specific point, but could easily be adapted for larger or smaller crossings.

Tensairity® Test Bridge

Rolf Luchsinger and Mauro Pedretti
Switzerland. 2004

Swiss inflatables firm Airlight has trademarked a new pneumatic technology entitled Tensairity, which uses a combination of low-pressure air beams, helical cabling and struts – inspired by the tensegrity structures of Buckminster Fuller and the floating compression ideas of artist Kenneth Snelson. The key principle of Tensairity is to use low-pressure air to stabilize compression elements against buckling. The basic Tensairity structure is a beam with the properties of a simple air beam (lightweight, fast set-up, low-cost installation and compact storage volume) but with the load-bearing capacity of conventional steel girders. These new lightweight composite beams have been proposed as bridge structures, temporary enclosures and wide-span roofs.

A Tensairity beam holding about
1300 kg (2866 lbs) of VW Golf.

Inflated Bridge

Military Engineering Experimental
Establishment (MEXE)
Cardington, UK. 1965

This prototype for an inflatable bridge spans 5.5 m (18 ft),
is 3-m (9-ft 10-in.) wide and is capable of carrying 1400 kg
(3086 lb). It is constructed from a three-ply fabric, made airtight
through the application of coats of rubber and neoprene.
The bridge beam is created with a series of internal fabric
diaphragms running longitudinally and acting as webs to keep
the top and bottom skins a fixed distance apart. Wires are
bonded to the lower skin to help resist tension and the traversable
deck is made with a series of individual timber slats which,
when the structure deflects, butt together to take compression.
The inflation pressure is just 13 kPa (1.8 psi) – the average domestic
car tyre is generally inflated to a pressure of 200 kPa (30 psi).

Lightweight Modular Causeway System (LMCS)

US Army Engineer Research
and Development Center (ERDC)
Global. 2008

This bridging system was developed by the research command of the US Army Corps of Engineers, who were looking for innovative ways to adapt and apply military technologies to humanitarian assistance and disaster-relief operations. The LMCS, when fielded, provides a versatile capability for military and disaster-response planners. Its shallow, floating deck is ideal for offloading vehicles from ship to shore. Each module of the system is 6-m (4-ft 11-in.) long and 3-m (9-ft 10-in.) wide and is supported by two 1.5-m (4-ft 11-in.) diameter pneumatic floats. The floats are low pressure, at about 6 kPa (1 psi) but can support in excess of 59,000 kg (65 tons). The system requires just 30 cm (11.75 in.) of water depth in an unladen state and is considerably lighter than a traditional pontoon bridge equivalent.

Lightweight Modular
Causeway System during
a trial assembly in Alaska.

FiDU Bridge
Oskar Zieta and Philipp Dohmen
ETH Zurich. 2007

The FiDU footbridge was developed
as a research project and collaboration
between Oskar Zieta and students of
architecture from the Swiss Federal
Institute of Technology (ETH Zurich) in
2007. FiDU is an acronym, it stands for
Freier Innen Druck Umformung (Free
Inner Pressure Reshaping). The bridge
has a span of 6 m (19 ft 8 in.) and
weighs only 174 kg (383 lb), which is an
impressive span-to-weight ratio achieved
with sheet steel. The predicted support
capacity of 500 kg (1102 lb) was easily
surpassed during stress testing, and
the maximum load, of 1850 kg (4078
lb), exceeded all expectations, giving
the FiDU bridge a 1:10 weight-to-load-
bearing ratio. The bridge is fabricated
from 1 mm (0.06 in.) thick sheet steel and
inflated with 40 kPa (5.8 psi) of air from a
compressor. The air is used to inflate the
two steel 'pillow' beams and the cross-
spanning deck elements. Zieta originally
worked with inflated steel furniture, such
as his Plopp stool (see p.132), and has also
developed other structural components,
such as columns, using the same
air-forming process.

The FiDU footbridge during
stress testing.

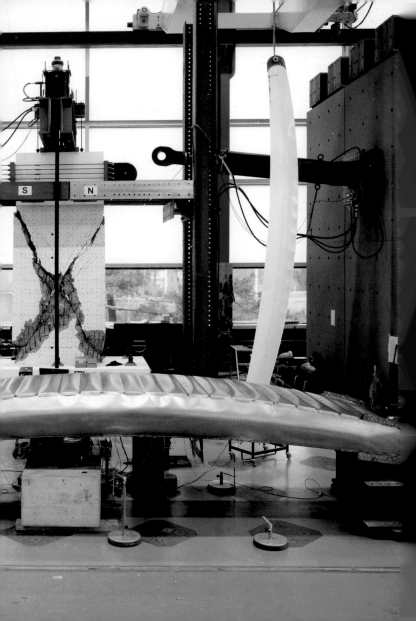

Uniboom® X
Markleen
Global. 2013

Containment booms are used in the event of oil spills on water
where they can temporarily prevent the spread of the spillage
while the pollutant is skimmed from the water's surface.
Uniboom X is a rapid-deployment boom system. The booms
are filled with compressed air during deployment when they
are unrolled from a large ship- or land-based reel. Over 400 m
(1312 ft) of the Uniboom X system can be deployed and made
fully operational within 15 minutes.

Tetraflot
Gilles Ebersolt
Various. 1980

Tetraflot is a structural system of interconnected low-pressure
air beams that uses a tetrahedral geometry for structural stability.
Ebersolt has used this system to create floating buoys
(pictured here), land-based event structures and ice sleds.

The Tetraflot floating buoy system.

AIR: MOVEMENT

2.1 / PNEUMATIC BUILDING SKINS

The use of air not simply to support a fabric structure, but to mediate environmental factors such as heating and cooling through dynamic solar shading and 'breathable' membranes, is still a relatively unexplored area of building science. The air cushion skins pioneered by Ben Morris of Vector Foiltec (see pp.12, 54 & 55) offer a clue to the future development of this field, where multilayered or multicellular skins can behave and be controlled dynamically with plenums and pockets of differential air pressure and density. Nikolaus Laing's pioneering work with dynamically active inflated skins remains largely unexplored by the construction industry and using a fabric multilayered skin for the atmospheric control of buildings is still perceived as highly ambitious.

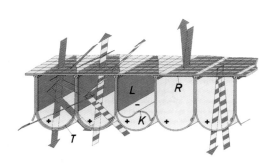

Environmentally Adaptive Pneumatic skin – wall element with pneumatically operated folding film K inside the air chamber L, on the left in 'transmission' position T, on the right in 'reflection' position R. (Markings: Yellow = transparent film; green = reflecting metal coating; red arrows = solar radiation; dotted arrows = ground radiation. From *The Use of Solar and Sky Radiation for Air Conditioning of Pneumatic Structures*, Nikolaus Laing, pp. 163–177, 1st International Colloquium on Pneumatic Structures (International Association for Shell Structures – IASS) University of Stuttgart, 1967.

Environmentally Adaptive Pneumatic skin

Nikolaus Laing

1967

*'A new "dynamic" method ... based on radiation physics,
capable of using solar energy for heating and the heat sink
effect of space for cooling.'*

NIKOLAUS LAING

During the proliferation of lightweight construction technologies
towards the end of the 1960s, German scientist Nikolaus Laing
became interested in the development of pneumatic enclosures
with dynamic and operable climatic skins. Laing was particularly
interested in how multilayered membranes could harness
solar radiation to create natural cooling and 'air conditioning'
effects. Laing's thinking was to develop dynamic wall designs
to maintain a physiologically acceptable temperature range
within an air-supported structure through the use of controllable
reflective and insulating fabric skins. This highly experimental
work can now be understood in the context of biomimetics,
a new branch of engineering, which takes its inspiration from
natural systems and their analogues. His dynamic skin is breathable
and reacts to external and internal temperature differentials,
much like human skin.

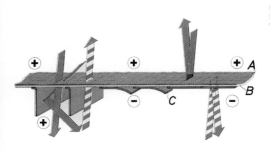

Environmentally Adaptive
Electrostatically Controlled Pneumatic
Wall – A = transparent conductive
outer layer; B = insulating, transparent
support layer; C = metallized
folding layer. If A and C are equally
charged electrically C assumes
a vertical position (thus realizing
full transparency); if the charge
is opposite, C will cling to B (thus
realizing complete reflection). From
*The Use of Solar and Sky Radiation
for Air Conditioning of Pneumatic
Structures*, Nikolaus Laing, pp. 163–177,
1st International Colloquium on
Pneumatic Structures (International
Association for Shell Structures – IASS)
University of Stuttgart, 1967.

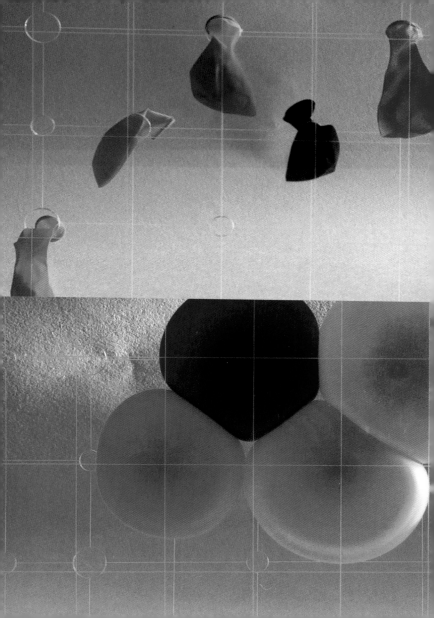

Pneumatic facade system developed by Near See Ng at the University of Westminster. Concept design for a responsive facade system using elastomeric air-filled balloons sandwiched between two glass screens. The expanding and contracting 'lungs' act as a solar control and as heat-capture vessels, trapping pockets of warm air.

Pneumatic-elastic building skin by Richard Northcroft at the University of Westminster. A series of individually actuated pneumatic cells create a kinetic flooring system.

2.2 / AIR MUSCLES, AIR SPRINGS & AIRBAGS

The use of air as a structural medium does not have to be exclusively for the forming of structural envelopes. The development of air muscles and air springs shows how engineered, air-filled components can be used mechanically as actuators, springs, hinges and isolators. Air springs are not a new invention and are widely used in the transportation industry as an alternative to heavier and less adaptive steel springs. Air muscles are a relatively new invention, their development owing much to the growing interest in biomimicry and the development of engineering solutions through the study of biological analogy. Airbags are commonly used as an automatic safety device in vehicles and are now featured in the body protectors worn by equestrian competitors in cross-country eventing. Airbags can also be used with a slower, more controlled deployment to lift heavy objects or to 'right' vehicles.

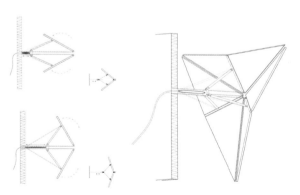

Movable facade project at the University of Westminster by Sarah Shuttleworth, using an air muscle actuator.

Air Muscle
Shadow Robot Company
2003

Air muscles are a type of actuator that provide a 'pulling' force similar to that of a biological muscle. A coaxial sleeve around a membrane restricts its cross-sectional inflation and thus 'pulls' the two muscle ends together with the addition of compressed air. The Shadow Robot Company's 30-mm (1⅛-in.) diameter air muscle will contract by up to 37 per cent of its original length and can produce forces of 700 N (516 ft lb) at pressures of only a few bar. Air muscles are lightweight and have no stiction (static friction), so have an instant and smooth response.

The force the muscle provides decreases as it contracts, and the first few per cent of the contraction is very powerful indeed. The simplest use of an air muscle is to have it move a lever. One muscle pulls the lever in one direction, and a spring can return it. Two muscles will allow the lever to be pulled in either direction, with considerable force. Because the muscle contracts over a known distance, it can be used to provide a safe movement: there is no need to ensure that the lever is not going to be pulled beyond its end-stop.

The Shadow muscle hand contains an integrated bank of 40 air muscles actuating 24 joints, allowing a direct mapping from human to robotic movement.

Air Springs
Firestone Industrial Products Company
1939

Air springs are engineered pneumatic devices that comprise
elastomeric bellows with metal end closures. They are
frictionless, sealed and require little maintenance. Air springs
are commonly used for cushioning against vibration, noise
or shock, but can also be employed as actuators for lifting
and in manufacturing processes such as forming presses.
Their advantage over pneumatic or hydraulic cylinders is fewer
moving parts and thus fewer leaks and replacement seals.
When used as springs for air-suspension systems in cars, trucks
and trains, the relative air pressure can be adjusted between
the 'springs' for a smooth ride.

Cutaway of a Firestone air spring.

Yahoo Truck
Adam Kalkin
Not Realised. 2008

Airbags are now standard safety devices in cars to cushion passengers in the event of a crash or sudden stop. Adam Kalkin has employed the aesthetic of a giant airbag for his Yahoo Truck project. The Yahoo Truck is a mobile showroom and Wi-Fi lounge. Disguised as a regular 12-m (39-ft) long shipping container towed by an articulated rig, the vehicle is transformed when hydraulic legs tip the container sideways, while two huge 'airbags' deploy to cushion its fall. Deflation of the giant cushions leaves the container having rotated a full 90 degrees, the erstwhile roof revealed as a fully glazed Yahoo storefront. The process is reversed by reinflating the 'airbags' until the trailer is righted – then it is ready to head off to another location.

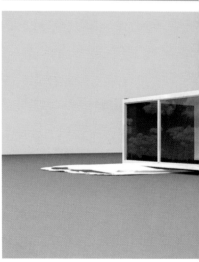

2.3 / TRANSPORTATION

The use of air in transportation has long been explored.
Air has notably been used as a propellant in the
pneumatic rail systems invented and trialled in the late
1800s, such as the Crystal Palace atmospheric railway,
and more recently in US entrepreneur Elon Musk's
speculative Hyperloop rail system. Alternatively,
air can be employed as an interstitial medium, utilizing
the hovercraft principle demonstrated in Jack Vaughen's
AirBarge system of floating decks (see p.106). The
artist Graham Stevens, while exploring the relationship
between man and nature, invented a unique bridging
system of inflated polythene which allows you to walk
on water (opposite), whereas Gilles Ebersolt's Ballule
(see p.102) has enabled this singular designer to traverse
some of the world's most challenging terrain.

Stevens looks down the length of his Hovertube sculpture

Hovertube
Graham Stevens
Cornwall, UK. 1970

'The purpose of creating events such as Walking on Air or Walking on Water is to explore the relationship between people and their environment.'

GRAHAM STEVENS

An extraordinary set of pneumatic artworks, started in the mid 1960s, saw Graham Stevens walk on water in a polythene cube and traverse land and water (both above and below the surface) in his Hovertube project. Hovertube is an air-supported structure; a transparent polythene tube that allows you to literally walk on water and, when deployed on land, can bridge rough terrain with the aid of pneumatic integrity. As well as the beautiful image created by the 402-m (1318-ft) long prototype in Cornwall, UK, in 1970 (see over), captured as part of Stevens's 1971 film *Atmosfields*, this human transportation tube would seem to have any number of practical applications.

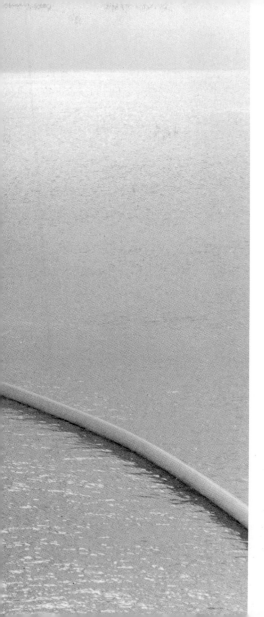

The fully deployed Hovertube in Cornwall, UK, 1970. Graham Stevens explored commercial applications for the Hovertube as a lightweight bridge and a flexible causeway between ships and land. Stevens also designed a Hovertube with two continuous pressurized chambers which could be 'steered' with the play of positive and negative pressure between the two chambers.

The Ballule
Gilles Ebersolt
Worldwide. 1974

In 1974, inspired by the work of a group of Dutch plastic artists called the Event Structures Research Group, the French architect and inventor Gilles Ebersolt decided to make an all-terrain spherical inflatable. Ebersolt's aim was the descent of the Cadélioque gorge at Vébron, southern France, in an inflatable object. In June 1977, Ebersolt demonstrated his first prototype of the Ballule, a spherical form of specially cut and welded transparent PVC plastic with an inner, inhabitable sphere tied to the outer skin using an evenly distributed set of parachute cords. The interstitial space between the membranes was inflated to a low pressure to create a type of air-cell structure. The Ballule attracted much publicity and Ebersolt continued to develop new iterations of his invention, including a giant 6-m (19-ft 18-in.) diameter version, which he used to descend Mount Fuji, and a version that featured in the 1991 Jackie Chan film *Operation Condor*. Ebersolt's invention continues to be much imitated.

Tensairity® Kite
Rolf Luchsinger and Joep Breuer
Various. 2009

Manned and unmanned aircraft that make
use of inflatable wings have previously
been constructed and successfully tested.
These include the Goodyear Inflatoplane
(1959) and Daniel Perkins' human-powered
prototype Reluctant Phoenix (1966).
However, the limited load-bearing
capacity of inflatable wings has restricted
the aspect ratio of this wing type.
By introducing the concept of Tensairity,
whereby the buckling of inflatable
beams is resisted using additional cables,
this structural deficiency is overcome.
The introduction of struts and cables
significantly increases the stiffness and
load capacity of the structure and the
latest prototype kite, or wing, has a span
of 8 m (26 ft) and a surface area of
11 square m (118 square ft).

AirBarge

Jack Vaughen and AirBarge
Various. 1959

Using the hovercraft technology pioneered by English engineer Christopher Cockerell in the 1950s, the 'air caster' system was developed in the 1960s by a number of industrial designers, such as Jack Vaughen, who created a range of transportation products called AirBarge. Air casters are used for moving heavy loads and, unlike wheels, are omnidirectional, with ease of movement in any lateral direction for manoeuvring in tight spaces. They provide a virtually frictionless bearing using a thin plenum of air, allowing a 500 kg (1102 lbs) load to be pushed or pulled with approximately 0.5 N (1 ft lbf) of force. Air casters could be classified as air-supporting structures – as opposed to air-supported structures – since tons of weight can literally be supported with a low-pressured 'air cushion'.

Another reason air casters are good for lifting heavy weights is that their greater surface area helps to distribute the weight being moved, which avoids point loading and thus damage to a floor surface or structure. Air casters are mostly used in industry to move large machine parts and manufactured objects around factories, but they have also been used to move large sculptures.

Jack Vaughen photographed in the 1960s with his patented range of AirBarge air casters.

A number of air casters are combined to form a 'levitating' plank with a support frame, used here for lifting large aeronautical components.

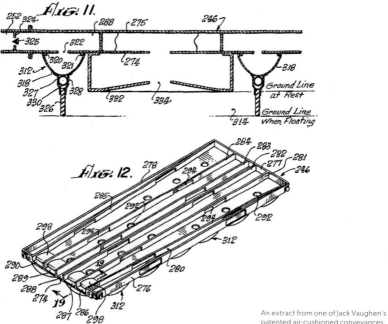

An extract from one of Jack Vaughen's patented air-cushioned conveyances.

AIR: DESIGNING
AND FABRICATING

3.1 / SOAP BUBBLES AS A DESIGN TOOL

Soap bubbles are physical illustrations of a minimal surface. A minimal surface can be described as a surface with equal pressure on the inside and the outside. A soap film obtained by dipping a wire-frame-bounded closed shape into a soapy solution will produce a minimal surface. This soap film 'form finding' process was used by Frei Otto in the design of his tensile fabric structures. Similarly, an analysis of soap bubbles can help to inform the design of intersecting surfaces of air-pressurized spherical forms or bubbles.

The spherical shape of a soap bubble is created by surface tension. The tension causes the bubble to form a sphere, as a sphere has the smallest possible surface area for a given volume. A soap bubble, due to the difference in outside and inside pressure, is a surface of constant mean curvature. When two soap bubbles merge, the bubbles will adopt the shape with the smallest possible surface area. With bubbles of a similar size, their common wall will be flat. Smaller bubbles, having a higher internal pressure, will bulge into larger bubbles. Where three or more bubbles meet, they organize themselves so that only three bubble walls meet along a line. Since the surface tension is the same in each of the three surfaces, the three angles between them must be equal to 120 degrees. Two merged soap bubbles provide the optimum way of enclosing two given volumes of air of different sizes with the least surface area. This has been termed the 'double bubble' theorem.

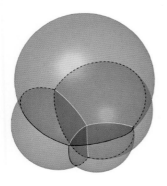

Researcher Mihail-Andrei Jipa, studying plateau angle conditions, illustrates how three soap films meet smoothly at equal angles of 120 degrees along a curve. Four such curves meet smoothly at equal angles of approximately 109 degrees.

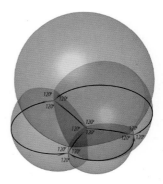

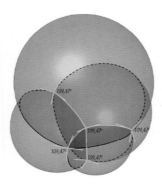

A detailed photographic study of
soap bubbles and soap films can help
the designer to 'find form' and define
minimal surfaces.

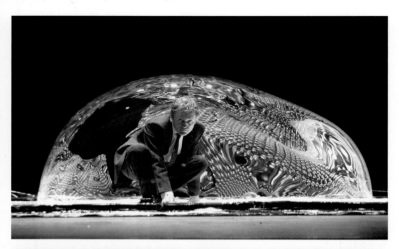

Spanish performance artist Pep Bou
sits inside one of his bubble sculptures
made with soap and water and (below)
creates a series of interlocking soap-film
bubbles at the annual Quebec City
Summer Festival.

3.2 / AIR-FORMED STRUCTURES

Inflated and air-supported structures require continuous air pressure to maintain their shape and structural properties. What if you could form a shape with air (in the way that you inflate a balloon) and then freeze and solidify that shape? This was the innovation of Italian architect Dante Bini, who had the idea of lifting wet concrete with an air-inflated membrane until the concrete form set solid and no longer required air to stand (opposite). The Concrete Canvas Shelter by Brewin and Crawford uses the same principle (see p.124), but innovates in its material use. The University of Maine's Bridge-in-a-Backpack (see p.122) also uses air to form a structure but, in this instance, the series of hollow composite tubes are then used as permanent formwork in themselves, as bridge arches. The Blackpool Wind Shelters by McChesney (see p.128) are not so much formed by air, but shaped by airflows to create dynamic rotating shelters.

Binishells brochure from 1967.

Binishell
Dante Bini
Various. 1965

For more than 40 years, Italian architect Dante Bini has dedicated his professional life to the development of what he calls 'automated construction technologies'. In 1965, in Bologna, Italy, he successfully constructed a 12 x 6 m (39 x 20 ft) hemispherical concrete shell structure in just three hours, using the unique pneumatic formwork of a giant balloon. This first prototype had some teething problems, however, particularly the uneven distribution of the wet concrete caused by an unpredictable asymmetric inflation. Improvements were made and in 1967, at New York's Columbia University, Bini demonstrated the construction of another large-scale Binishell, which took just two hours. For this first US prototype

he used a complex web of helical 'springs' with steel reinforcement bars threaded through their middle, which allowed for a geometrically controlled inflation and thus uniform concrete distribution. For this demonstration, and subsequent Binishell structures, an additional external PVC membrane was used to allow for the vibration and compaction of the concrete, post-inflation. More than 1,500 Binishells were constructed throughout the world between 1970 and 1990 with diameters of between 12 and 36 m (39 and 118 ft), and with a varying elliptical section. Binishells have been fabricated as houses, schools, sports facilities and as industrial storage units.

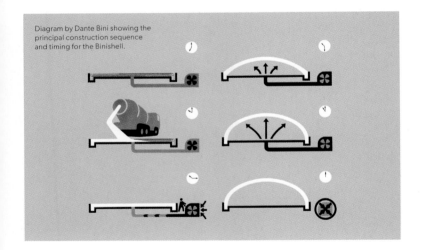

Diagram by Dante Bini showing the principal construction sequence and timing for the Binishell.

Construction sequence for the 18-m (59-ft) diameter Binishell for Ashbury Public School Administration Building, New South Wales, Australia. A unique system of springs traverse the circular concrete slab, with reinforcement rods inside the springs. The reinforcement is laid over a carefully pleated pattern-cut membrane. Concrete is then distributed evenly over the inflatable membrane and reinforcement.

A PVC membrane is laid over the concrete to help control its distribution and the quality of the finish.

Inflation via a small air-pumping plant starts to lift the concrete.

When inflation is complete, 'vibration carts' are pulled around and across the surface of the wet concrete dome to compact and consolidate the thin concrete shell.

The finished dome is kept inflated for at least 24 hours, until the structure has become sufficiently stable.

View of the Villa Antonioni, Costa
Paradiso, Sardinia, Italy, 1970. Dante
Bini designed this house for the film
director Michelangelo Antonioni
and the actress Monica Vitti.

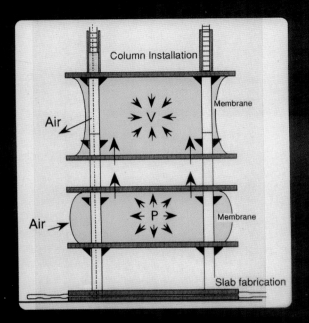

AIR LIFT UP SYSTEM
A lift up construction method
utilizing air pressure as a lifting force

Column Installation

Membrane

Air

V

Air

P

Membrane

Slab fabrication

**Principal Construction Processes
of the Air Lift up System**

Diagram of a vertical construction
system using positive and negative
pressure to 'push up' and 'pull up'
concrete slabs, one of the systems
developed by Dante Bini while working
with the Japanese Shimizu Corporation.

Spatium Gelatum
Zbigniew Oksiuta
Various. 2003

Artist Zbigniew Oksiuta argues that most of what is described as organic, fluid or dynamic architecture is no such thing, and its relationship with biology is limited or analogical only. His Spatium Gelatum project is designed to explore new architectures and their relationship with biological sciences. According to Oksiuta, 'the space of the Spatium Gelatum will possess different tastes, smells and be edible'. To create his spatial forms, Oksiuta draws on the concept of isopycnic systems (neutral buoyancy); the technology of lava lamps; Frei Otto's work on the Pneu as one of nature's basic construction forms; and what he calls *Lane Kluski* technology or, roughly translated from Polish, 'the cooking of poached dumplings'. Initial prototypes have been fabricated with the biological polymer by-product gelatine using inflated PVC forms. The gelatine is applied as a series of thin liquid layers and when the skin is thick enough and the polymer has set, the air pressure is reduced and the inner formwork is removed.

The Spatium Gelatum enclosures use air-inflated PVC supports while they are fabricated.

Bridge-in-a-Backpack

Advanced Infrastructure Technologies /
University of Maine's Advanced Structures
and Composites Center (AEWC)
Maine, USA. 2003

This composite arch bridge, nicknamed 'Bridge-in-a-Backpack',
is a lightweight, corrosion-resistant system for short- to medium-
span bridge construction using fibre-reinforced polymer (FRP)
composite arches that act as reinforcement and formwork for
cast-in-place concrete. Developed out of a partnership between the
University of Maine and the Maine Department of Transportation
after a need to replace ageing infrastructure had been identified,
the patent-pending technology can literally be folded up and
packed into a small bag. The arches are made of woven
carbon-fibre tubes, which are inflated, held in a simple jig and
then resin-infused and cured. The arches are easily transportable,
rapidly deployable, and do not require the heavy equipment
or large crews needed to handle the weight of traditional
construction materials. Anchored side-by-side in footings on
opposite sides of the span, the arches are subsequently filled
with concrete and covered with composite panels that support
the roadway. This new technology can compete on cost with
concrete and steel, and several such bridges have already
been successfully installed in the US.

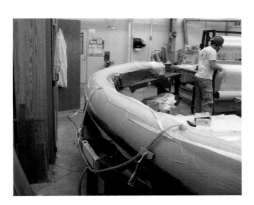

The Bridge-in-a-Backpack is unrolled
as a fibre sleeve, inflated into a tube
shape and infused with resin to harden
it into a lightweight beam.

The lightweight hollow beams
are lifted into place.

The arches are then concreted
into foundations.

Concrete Canvas Shelter

Peter Brewin and William Crawford
Various. 2004

Concrete Canvas Shelters are rapidly deployable hardened
shelters that require only water and air for construction. The
structures have major advantages over conventional tented
shelters: they provide a rigid structure from day one and they
offer excellent environmental protection and structural longevity
(they have a design life of over 10 years). One of the key
technologies of the shelter is the use of air inflation to create a
surface that is optimized for compressive loading. This allows a
thin-walled concrete structure to be formed, which is both robust
and lightweight. The skin of the shelter consists of a revolutionary
cement-based composite fabric, known as 'Concrete Canvas',
which is bonded to the outer surface of a plastic inner lining
that forms a hut-shaped structure once inflated.

Concrete Canvas Shelters are supplied folded in rot-proof sacks
within heat-treated timber crates. An electric fan is used to inflate
the plastic inner lining to lift the structure until it is self-supporting.
The shelter is then hydrated by being sprayed with water
(non-potable and seawater may be used). The Concrete Canvas
cures in the shape of the inflated inner and is ready to use in
only 24 hours. Access holes can later be cut through the skin
to allow for the installation of services.

Concrete Canvas Shelters, and the material Concrete Canvas,
were invented by Peter Brewin and William Crawford while
studying Industrial Design Engineering at Imperial College and
the Royal College of Art in London.

The Concrete Canvas Shelter
is unfolded and inflation
is started.

The fully inflated shelter is sprayed with water to hydrate the cementitious fabric.

The Concrete Canvas is cured and the shelter is ready to use 24 hours later.

Blackpool Wind Shelters
Ian McChesney and Atelier One
Blackpool, UK. 2006

Following a successful competition entry, Ian McChesney
was commissioned to design two rotating wind shelters for
Blackpool's South Shore Promenade. The shelters are designed
to rotate according to the prevailing wind direction to shield
the occupants from the elements. The shape was born out of
a distillation of the key requirements: a vane, which will turn the
structure, and a baffle, that will shelter the inhabitant from the
wind. Extensive testing and development work was carried
out to establish the performance of the shelters, culminating
in the manufacture of a full-sized working prototype. The final
shelters are 8 m (26 ft) tall and manufactured from resilient
Duplex stainless steel. They sit on 4-m (13-ft) diameter turntables,
which incorporate dampers to control the speed of rotation.

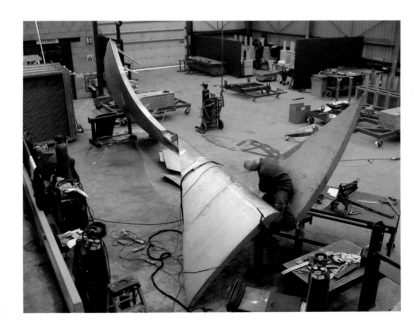

Above: Early test model checking
the wind-activated rotation.

Left: Fabrication of the
'wind-shaped' shelters.

3.3 / AIR-FORMED FURNITURE, FIXTURES AND FASHION

Air has been used as both a forming and supportive medium in the fields of furniture and fashion. Oskar Zieta's Plopp stool (below) is a great example of air-formed furniture, while Jamie Wolfond's Emergency Bench (see p.138) enjoys its pneumatic heritage as a miniature air beam. The nascent use of air in fashion demonstrates how structures can be formed and maintained by air and how its insulative properties may be put to both practical and stylistic use.

FiDU
Oskar Zieta and Philipp Dohmen
ETH Zurich. 2003

Sheet metal has previously been shaped into three-dimensional forms by processes such as beating, folding (on a brake press), spinning and wheeling – but now it can also be formed with high-pressure inflation. Architect Oskar Zieta and materials scientist Philipp Dohmen, both researchers at Zurich's Swiss Federal Institute of Technology (ETH) have devised a process called Free Internal Pressure Reshaping (FiDU). Thin sheet metal is welded together along seams, and then inflated with high-pressure air through a pre-installed valve. The first product that the duo produced with the FiDU process was the Plopp stool. Remarkably strong, after inflation the stool can support 2500 kg (2.75 tons), despite being light enough to be easily lifted with only one hand. The invention is also material efficient: the welded sheets can be flat-packed and shipped 100 to a palette, then inflated by a local fabricator closer to their final destination. In 2010 Zieta demonstrated his FiDU Blow and Roll technology at the Victoria and Albert Museum, London, by displaying rolls of specially fabricated, flat steel 'tube' that were inflated to create a series of sheet-steel arches.

The compressed air formed
Plopp stool, very strong, but light

Demonstration of the Blow and Roll concept, where a flat 'tube' fabricated from two thin sheets of steel is literally blown into shape.

FiDU Blow and Roll technology in the
courtyard of the Victoria and Albert
Museum, London.

Emergency Bench
Jamie Wolfond
New York, USA. 2014

One of a new generation of designer-makers exploring specialist fabrication and manufacturing processes, Brooklyn-based Canadian designer Jamie Wolfond has created a three-person 'emergency' bench. The components include a welded-fabric inflatable cylinder (made by a white-water raft manufacturer), cast-bronze leg brackets and nylon straps. The bench can be inflated with a foot-pump or compressed air. Air is the major structural component.

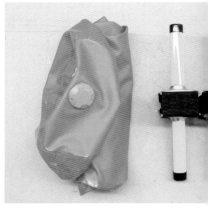

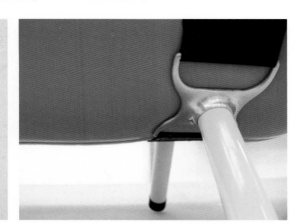

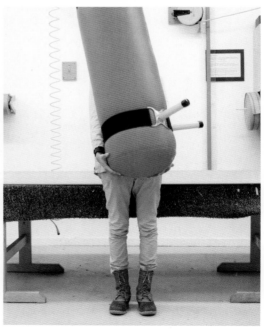

Blow

Theo Möller
Halle, Germany. 2014

This inflatable light is a miniature air beam fabricated from two pulse-welded sheets of polyethylene, one of which has an aluminium coating to act as a reflector. A non-returnable valve holds the lamp in shape once inflated, creating a rigid strut, and the LED luminaires are contained inside. The pattern-cut nature of the design means that it comes in a variety of shapes and sizes, all of which are very lightweight. A 4-metre-long (13-ft) lamp weighs only 400 grams (14 oz).

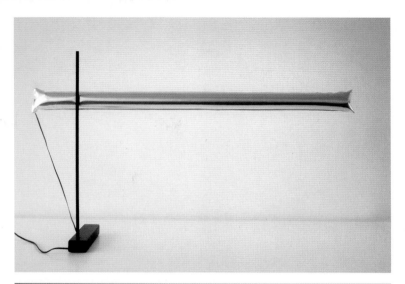

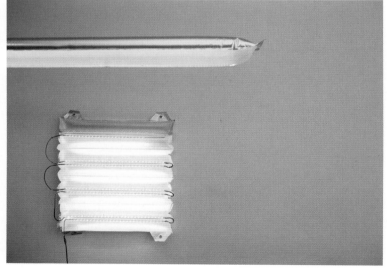

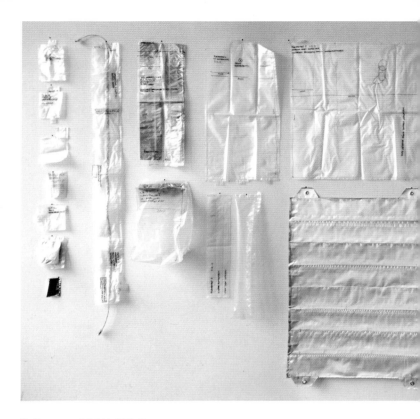

The Blow range of inflatable LED lights
made from inflated aluminium-coated
plastic membranes.

Inflatable Clothes
Flora McLean for House of Flora
London. 1995

This prototype ready-to-wear collection of pneumatic clothes was fabricated in collaboration with inflatable structures guru Nick Crosbie. The inflated elements variously give structure to a coat collar, hat brim or the hoop of a skirt. Using a process of high-frequency plastic welding, the tailoring and seaming of these garments is re-imagined to embrace new fabrication technologies and material developments. The inventiveness of fashion designers in the use and development of new materials and fabricating processes, coupled

with the fast turnaround of the fashion calendar, provides a great incubator of ideas that more architects would do well to embrace.

Air has been utilized in the footwear industry since the invention of Dr Klaus Märten's air-cushioned sole in the late 1940s, launched as Doc Martens AirWair in 1960. In 1987 Nike launched the Air Max range of training shoe, which featured a clearly visible cushion of trapped air in the sole.

Inflatable garments by Flora McLean,
Royal College of Art MA fashion
show, 1995.

Inflatable beach skirt
and bubble, 1996.

3.4 / MATERIALS WITH ADDED AIR

Lightness should be one of the great imperatives of the construction industry. Less weight equals less material, which equals less pollution. There are also other major benefits to be had from the use of aerated material, such as a reduction in thermal conductivity and a reduction in the dead weight of material, thus improving structural efficiency. While the aerated-concrete breeze block is not a new idea, the logic of introducing air into materials such as metals and polymers to form foams (highly specialized in the automotive and aerospace industries) holds much promise for the more slow-to-evolve business of constructing buildings.

Autoclaved Aerated Concrete (AAC)
Johan Axel Eriksson
Stockholm, Sweden. 1923

Autoclaved Aerated Concrete is a lightweight, precast building material that simultaneously provides structure, insulation and fire resistance. It is only 20 per cent of the weight of concrete. Quartz sand, lime and/or cement and water are used as a binding agent, along with aluminium powder. When AAC is mixed and cast in moulds several chemical reactions take place that give it its lightweight and thermal properties. Aluminium powder reacts with calcium hydroxide and water to form hydrogen. The hydrogen gas foams and, as a result, doubles the volume of the raw mix, creating gas bubbles up to 3 mm (0.12 in.) in diameter. At the end of the foaming process, the hydrogen escapes into the atmosphere and is replaced … by air.

Cobiax
Cobiax Technology Group
Switzerland. 2000

Even in the heavyweight world of reinforced concrete, products such as Cobiax can reduce the dead load of a concrete slab by 35–50 per cent by introducing holes (in the form of hollow plastic spheres) to the concrete mix. Cobiax is described as a voided biaxial slab, the recycled plastic spheres are sandwiched and held in place between reinforcement mesh. The success of

this system is that it uses conventional construction technology but, through the addition of air pockets formed by the inexpensive plastic spheres, a typical floor slab can be lightened and thus strengthened. There are various versions of this system, which use a variety of differently shaped void-formers – such as squashed lozenge shapes – to reduce the overall depth of the slab.

Image from John William Todd's
patent for Aerated Chocolate,
latterly known as Aero.

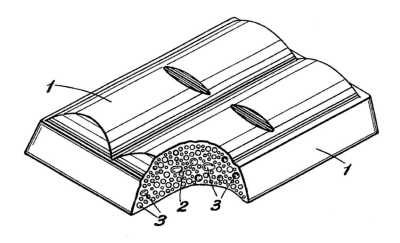

Aerated Chocolate

John William Todd for Rowntree's
York, UK. 1935

Launched as 'The New Chocolate' in 1935, Aero was invented
as a patented process '…characterized by the whole article, or
such parts, at lower temperatures, being in the form of a rigid
cellular or honeycomb structure readily visible to the eye'. While
the addition of air might suggest less chocolate, the 'aeration'
can also mean a dimensionally larger bar with the same amount
of chocolate; the confectioner's version of doing more with less,
or selling less for more.

Metal Foam

ERG Aerospace Corporation
California, USA. 1967

While their inclusion as 'air structures' might be stretching
the definition a little too far, it is true that one of the chief
characteristics of metal foams is their relative lightness.
Metal foam is very porous, with typically 75–90 per cent of its
volume consisting of air voids – making these ultralight materials,
weighing between 10–25 per cent of the weight of their non-
porous equivalents. A metal foam is a cellular structure consisting
of a solid metal (typically, but not exclusively, aluminium)
containing a large volume of gas-filled, or gas-generated, pores.
The pores can be sealed as a 'closed-cell' foam or made as an
'open-cell' foam in an interconnected network. Closed-cell
foams retain the fire resistance and recycling capability of other
metallic foams and have the added ability of being able to float
on water. One of the key applications of metal foams is their use
as heat exchangers, owing to their large surface area and
porosity. Due to the high cost of this material it is most typically
used in advanced technologies and manufacturing processes,
such as aerospace. Metal foams have been proposed as a
structural material and as a sheet material, but relative cost
has thus far restricted their use.

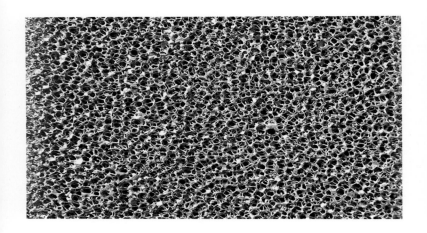

THE TECHNOLOGY
OF AIR

4.1 / AIR PRESSURE

The SI (International System of Units) unit of pressure
is the Pascal (Pa). 1 Pa = 1 N/m^2.

As the Pascal is an extremely small unit of measurement,
pressures in air structures are often described in kPa,
bar, psi, atmospheres or the height of a liquid column
(mm aq). Although the bar is a non-SI unit, 1 bar
represents the standard atmospheric pressure on
Earth and equates to 100,000 Pa or 100 kPa. The
measurement psi is an imperial measurement of lb.
per square inch and is often used as a measurement
for tyre pressure. For example, the tyres of a small
car might typically be inflated to 29 psi, which is 200
kPa or approximately 2 bars. In Mamoru Kawaguchi's
'Air-Supported' Orchid Conference pavilions (see p.18)
the air pressure was approximately 300 Pa in normal
conditions and increased to approximately 700 Pa to
resist strong winds or snow loads. In Kawaguchi's 'Air-
Inflated' Fuji Group pavilion (see p.33), where massive
inflated beams were used to create and maintain form,
the pressure inside the 4-m (13-ft) diameter interlocking
air beams was 9800 Pa (9.8 kPa). So while the pressure
of the air-beam structure of the Fuji Pavilion is significantly
higher than that of the air-supported structure, it is
still only a tenth of the pressure of a fully inflated FIFA
regulation football, which is 108 kPa (15.6 psi).

4.2 / KEY PEOPLE

Bini, Dante
After studying architecture in Florence, Italy, Dante Bini (b.1932) became interested in the technology of thin-shell concrete domes and was convinced that there must be new ways of forming these doubly curved shell structures. Inspired by the relative strength of a pneumatic, air-supported tennis dome, in 1964 Bini successfully constructed a 12-m (39-ft) diameter, 6-m (19-ft) high hemispherical concrete shell structure (Binishell) in three hours, lifting wet concrete using his patented pneumatic formwork. Bini has developed and patented a number of construction systems for building with air, including Minishell, Binix and Binistar.

Bird, Walter
Walter Bird (1912–2006) trained as an aeronautical engineer, graduating from MIT in 1934. At the end of World War II he joined the Cornell Aeronautical Laboratory in Buffalo, New York, where he directed the design and construction of the world's first air-supported radome in 1946. Several hundred of these radomes were subsequently built to protect radar antennas from extreme climate. In 1956 he established Birdair, which specialized in the design and manufacture of some of the world's largest and most complex air-supported structures and tensioned membranes. Walter Bird led this field through developments of materials and fabrication techniques and helped to popularize this rapidly developing new field.

Crosbie, Nick
Since setting up Inflate in 1995 Nick Crosbie has designed and manufactured a whole family of pneumatic structures, including the world's first inflatable eggcup, blow-up classrooms, inflatable changing rooms and huge pneumatic domes, walls and enclosures for temporary events. Crosbie has also developed a number of unique pneumatic structural systems, which include SuperCube, ExtremeDome and GrandeTurtle. Recently Crosbie has launched a system called AirClad for 'semi-permanent' inflatable architecture and cladding systems.

Kawaguchi, Mamoru
Mamoru Kawaguchi (b.1932) is a highly celebrated structural engineer and inventor of the deployable Pantadome structural system. He has worked with noted Japanese architects Arata Isozaki and Kenzo Tange. He was the engineer for the iconic Fuji Group Pavilion Expo '70 and the cable-reinforced air-supported structure of the 12th World Orchid Conference Pavilions, Tokyo, 1987, both designed by architect Yutaka Murata.

Lanchester, Frederick William
As well as earning his status as one of the key automotive engineers of his generation the inventor and polymath F.W. Lanchester (1868–1946) also found time to patent designs for air-supported structures. In his patent application from 1917 for *Construction of Tents for Field Hospitals, Depots, and Like Purposes*, he details the necessary foundations, airlocks and cable connections, and a note that the relative internal air pressure be raised in the event of high winds or snow load. In his later patent application of 1920 *Construction and Roofing of Buildings for Exhibitions and like Purposes*, Lanchester proposes a 300-m (984-ft) diameter cable-reinforced air-supported structure and states (with remarkable accuracy since proven), that 'The pressure required merely to sustain such a roof … is but a fraction of an inch water gauge and under ordinary circumstances half an inch (125 Pa) or an inch (250 Pa) water gauge is more than adequate to sustain the roof and impart a sufficient degree of rigidity.'

Otto, Frei
Frei Otto (b.1925) is an architect and pioneer of structural form-finding through the study of nature and biological design. In 1964 he founded the Institute of Lightweight Structures at the University of Stuttgart, which he directed until 1991. His groundbreaking and dextrous research is documented in numerous publications and in his body of built work and structural inventions over six decades. Otto studied the use of air as a structural medium, which he describes as the Pneu and he states …'The air hall is one of the very few fundamental innovations in building technology during the last 100 years.'

Price, Cedric

Cedric Price (1934–2003) was a highly influential British architect whose projects include Fun Palace (1960) and the Potteries Thinkbelt (1964). Price's work addresses issues of temporality, human comfort and design as a service industry sector. He presented a paper at the proceedings of the *1st International Colloquium on Pneumatic Structures*, Stuttgart 1967 and jointly founded the Lightweight Enclosures Unit (LEU) in 1969 with structural engineer Frank Newby. The LEU was established following a UK government-sponsored research programme. The work included '...research and design into the social, economic and structural development of lightweight enclosures'. In 1971 Newby and Price authored *Air Structures: A Survey*, published by Her Majesty's Stationery Office, a hitherto unsurpassed document of the history and technology of pneumatic structures.

Stevens, Graham

Graham Stevens (b.1944) is an artist who works across the domains of environmental art and architecture. Stevens began working with air structures and plastic membranes in the mid 1960s to produce single-colour surfaces exploring a saturated (colour) environment as an inhabited artwork: the structure formed by the air, the colour by the fabric. The success of these early prototypes encouraged Stevens and the then semi-derelict St. Katharine Docks became his studio for a series of extraordinary large-scale air sculptures, brilliantly captured on film by photographer Andrew Tweedie. Stevens became increasingly interested in the environmental potential of these lightweight architectures and in 1970 he developed an Atmospheric Raft (a buoyant structure) held aloft by the heat of the sun and documented in his film *Desert Cloud*, 1974.

INDEX

INDEX

PICTURE CREDITS